Most Provocative 20th Century Artworks

Heather Miller

Series Editor
Jeffrey D. Wilhelm

Much thought, debate, and research went into choosing and ranking the 10 items in each book in this series. We realize that everyone has his or her own opinion of what is most significant, revolutionary, amazing, deadly, and so on. As you read, you may agree with our choices, or you may be surprised — and that's the way it should be!

an imprint of

SCHOLASTIC

www.scholastic.com/librarypublishing

A Rubicon book published in association with Scholastic Inc.

Ru'bĭcon © 2007 Rubicon Publishing Inc.
www.rubiconpublishing.com

 is a trademark of The 10 Books

Associate Publishers: Kim Koh, Miriam Bardswich
Project Editor: Amy Land
Editor: Bettina Fehrenbach
Creative Director: Jennifer Drew
Project Manager/Designer: Jeanette MacLean
Graphic Designer: Brandon Köpke

The publisher gratefully acknowledges the following for permission to reprint copyrighted material in this book.

Every reasonable effort has been made to trace the owners of copyrighted material and to make due acknowledgment. Any errors or omissions drawn to our attention will be gladly rectified in future editions.

"A Priceless Find," excerpt from "The strange case of pop art: The cult of Andy Warhol highlights the wonderfully bizarre pop art movement, A Priceless Find." By Aidan Johnson. From Varsity Publications Inc. Permission courtesy of Varsity Publications Inc.

Cover image: *Marilyn* by Andy Warhol–Bildarchiv Preussischer Kulturbesitz/Art Resource, NY

Library and Archives Canada Cataloguing in Publication

Miller, Heather, 1943-
    The 10 most provocative 20th century artworks/Heather Miller.

Includes index.
ISBN 978-1-55448-483-6

    1. Readers (Elementary). 2. Readers—Arts. I. Title. II. Title: Ten most provocative 20th century artworks.

PE1117.M5575 2007   428.6   C2007-900577-2

1 2 3 4 5 6 7 8 9 10   10   16 15 14 13 12 11 10 09 08 07

Printed in Singapore

Contents

6

34

38

YOU CALL THAT ART?

Be prepared … You might be shocked by what you find in this book. Say goodbye to *Mona Lisa* and hello to the wacky world of modern art.

But what exactly is modern art? Well, just take a bunch of paint and throw it on a canvas — it doesn't matter where. Or better yet, just hang out in a room with a wild animal — yep, that counts as modern art, too. You can probably already see why some of the artworks in this book ticked people off. But these creations did a lot more than raise people's blood pressure.

The interesting thing about modern art is that it is provocative. It changed the way artists (and regular folks) thought about art. People started asking questions that they hadn't considered before. Artists started changing the way they created their work. Photography was new in the early 20th century and people realized that artists didn't have to paint or sculpt things exactly as they looked. This is when the expression "art is dead" arose. Paintings used to serve the purpose that photography does now.

In this book, we feature what we think are the 10 most provocative artworks of the 20th century. We feel that these artists used their creativity, originality, and courage to make a huge impact on contemporary art.

provocative: *causing a reaction such as anger, excitement, or curiosity*

WHAT IS THE MOST PROVOCATIVE MODERN ARTWORK?

Valley Curtain *by Christo and Jeanne-Claude, 1970–72*

Can you imagine spending just over two years to create a work of art that you intend to destroy shortly after you complete it? That's what Christo and Jeanne-Claude did with their installation art *Valley Curtain*, which was displayed in a Colorado canyon.

Christo and Jeanne-Claude are environmental artists who use both the rural and urban environment to create temporary works of art. They describe their art as a "gentle disturbance" to make people see the world with fresh eyes. The artists want people to have an intense

AIN

ARTISTS: Christo and Jeanne-Claude, both born 1935

MEDIUM: Woven nylon fabric

SIZE: 1,250 ft. wide with a height ranging from 365 ft. at each end to 182 ft. at the center

WHAT'S NEW: It took art out of the galleries and into the environment.

VALLEY CURTAIN–PHOTO: WOLFGANG VOLZ–©1972 CHRISTO

experience of art outside of museums and galleries. That's why they made *Valley Curtain* so big. You sure couldn't ignore it!

Valley Curtain was only on display for a very

short time and then it was gone forever. Today, because Christo and Jeanne-Claude have such an amazing global reputation, people flock to see their installations. They want to be part of a once-in-a-lifetime experience.

VALLEY CURTAIN

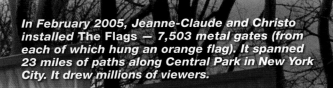

The Valley Curtain was anchored by extensive cabling.

BUT WHAT IS IT?

Valley Curtain was an environmental installation artwork. Installation art is art that can be made of any material in any given space. *Valley Curtain* consisted of an enormous bright orange curtain that was strung from one mountain to another across a valley in Grand Hogback, Rifle, Colorado. *Valley Curtain* was made out of nylon fabric, which weighed nine tons. It took 28 months to complete.

WHERE IS IT NOW?

Valley Curtain was intended to be displayed for at least a few weeks. Unfortunately, a huge windstorm forced the artists to start removing it just 28 hours after it was installed! There are many beautiful photographs of the curtain, but the actual artwork is gone forever.

WHAT'S UP WITH THESE ARTISTS?

Christo and Jeanne-Claude want to change the way people view their surroundings by turning the familiar into the unfamiliar. Their art is designed to give people a sense of urgency to see it because it will not last long.

FOOD FOR THOUGHT

Christo and Jeanne-Claude are fiercely protective of their artistic freedom, which is why they finance everything themselves. *Valley Curtain* cost about $400,000 to complete. The artists sold everything they had to finance their project.

In February 2005, Jeanne-Claude and Christo installed The Flags — 7,503 metal gates (from each of which hung an orange flag). It spanned 23 miles of paths along Central Park in New York City. It drew millions of viewers.

? Is there something you would like to do so much that you would be willing to sell everything you own just to make it happen? Explain your answer.

The Expert Says...

"Their work was highly influential on artists of my generation … interested in working outside the gallery and studio. Their projects were created for the masses, in the landscape."

— Christine Bechstein, artist and sculpture professor

ENVIRONMENTALISTS, ARTISTS, OR BOTH: YOU DECIDE!

After reading this article, decide whether Christo and Jeanne-Claude are ruining or helping the environment.

Some people complain that the projects Christo and Jeanne-Claude create will hurt the environment. What they don't realize is that after every project, absolutely everything is removed and recycled. The artists display their art for a short period of time so it's less likely to have an impact on the environment. All the sites, except in Florida, were restored to their original condition. In Florida, where Christo and Jeanne-Claude did an artwork called *Surrounded Islands*, they removed 40 tons of garbage before they started. You can be sure that Christo and Jeanne-Claude did not return these islands to their original condition.

Most environmentalists, such as the Audubon Society and the Sierra Club, support Christo and Jeanne-Claude's work because it draws attention to the environment in a big way.

Tickled pink! In 1983, Christo and Jeanne-Claude created Surrounded Islands. Eleven islands were covered in nearly two million square feet of polypropene, a plastic material.

Quick Fact

Christo and Jeanne-Claude were both born on the same day in the same year but in different countries. How cool is that?

Take Note

We ranked the *Valley Curtain* #10 on our list because it came late in the 20th century and had less influence on modern art than the other works on this list. It is important because it took art out of the galleries and influenced how people thought about art and society.

• Do you agree with the environmentalists who say that the environment benefits from Christo and Jeanne-Claude's artwork? Explain your answer.

5   4   3   2   1

⑨ HARRAN II

> "I don't like to say I have given my life to art. I prefer to say art has given me my life."
> — FRANK STELLA

*H*arran II is one of many ideas Frank Stella played around with in the 1960s. He was trying to push the limits of painting at a time when all the critics were saying painting was dead. Even though the critics were very powerful in the 1960s, Stella didn't agree with them. He kept coming up with new ideas to prove his point. What a rebel!

Stella's work introduced a way of making paintings in a style other than the very popular abstract expressionism (a movement where artists typically applied paint rapidly and with force in an effort to show feelings and emotions). His first major paintings to rock the art world were his *Black Paintings* in 1958. These dramatically changed the way art developed in the 1960s. Most critics say Stella's *Black Paintings* were the beginning of minimalism, which is an art movement based on extreme simplicity and objectivity.

---

abstract: *portraying feelings rather than recognizable objects*

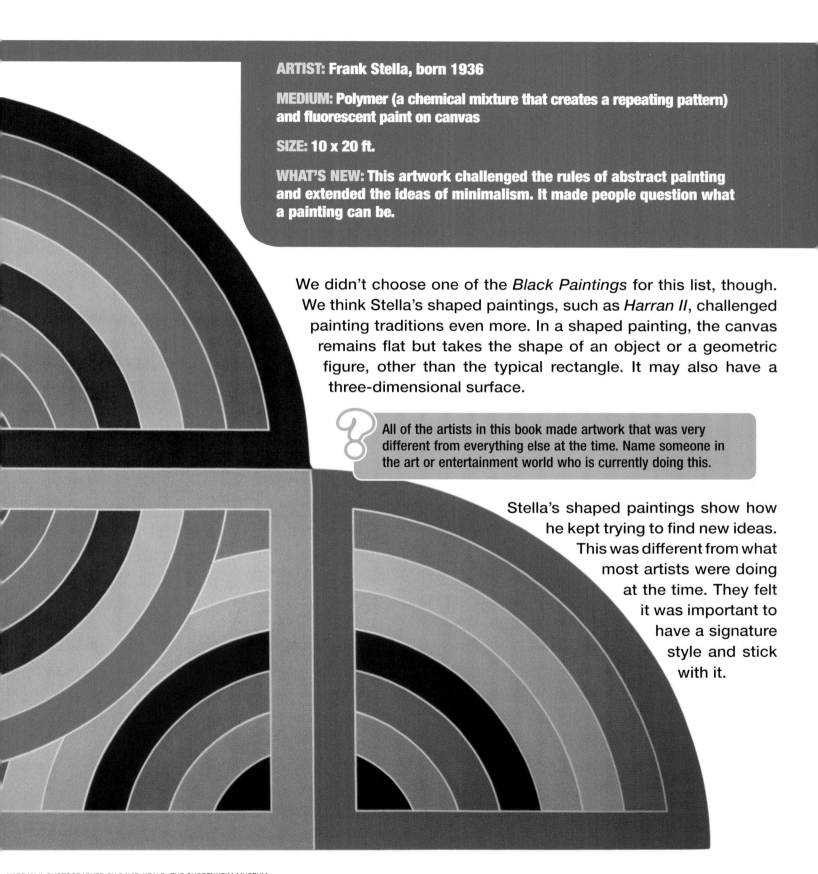

ARTIST: Frank Stella, born 1936

MEDIUM: Polymer (a chemical mixture that creates a repeating pattern) and fluorescent paint on canvas

SIZE: 10 x 20 ft.

WHAT'S NEW: This artwork challenged the rules of abstract painting and extended the ideas of minimalism. It made people question what a painting can be.

We didn't choose one of the *Black Paintings* for this list, though. We think Stella's shaped paintings, such as *Harran II*, challenged painting traditions even more. In a shaped painting, the canvas remains flat but takes the shape of an object or a geometric figure, other than the typical rectangle. It may also have a three-dimensional surface.

All of the artists in this book made artwork that was very different from everything else at the time. Name someone in the art or entertainment world who is currently doing this.

Stella's shaped paintings show how he kept trying to find new ideas. This was different from what most artists were doing at the time. They felt it was important to have a signature style and stick with it.

Harran II *by Frank Stella, 1967*

HARRAN II

BUT WHAT IS IT?

Harran II is a large, oddly shaped painting made up of a full circle and two overlapping half circles that have been created using a giant protractor. Parts of the painting seem to come forward while other parts go backward.

WHERE IS IT NOW?

The Solomon R. Guggenheim Museum in New York City is home to this painting. The museum's mission is to preserve and exhibit an art collection that reflects the most important artistic achievements of the 20th and 21st centuries.

WHAT'S UP WITH THIS ARTIST?

In *Harran II*, which is part of the *Protractor Series*, Stella decided to give a shape to the actual canvas. He wanted to eliminate all signs of brushstrokes from the painting. The outside shape of the canvas determined the actual content of the painting.

FOOD FOR THOUGHT

When Stella first started making his shaped canvases, critics and other artists said he was finished — this art form was not popular at the time. He proved them wrong. Today he is now one of the most successful artists of the late 20th century. In 2004, *ARTnews* magazine listed Frank Stella as one of the top 10 most expensive living artists, which means that his paintings sell for some of the highest prices.

Frank Stella peeks out from a mural he created for the Princess of Wales Theatre in Toronto, Canada, in 1993.

The Expert Says...

"This exhibition [at Harvard University Art Museums, 2006] offers new insight into the creative process of one of the most influential postwar American artists. ... These pieces were created ... at a moment of exuberant experimentation."

— Thomas W. Lentz, Elizabeth and John Moors Cabot, Harvard University Art Museums

exuberant: *enthusiastic; joyful*

Stella and the ART EXPERT

Read this article about Stella's slow rise to fame.

Frank Stella poses in an artistically created hat.

In 1959, art historian Thomas Hoving, who had just been hired as a curator for The Museum of Modern Art in New York City, visited Frank Stella at his studio. He liked Stella's *Black Paintings* and asked the artist how much one would cost. Stella decided the painting was worth $75. Hoving said he was just newly married and would have to ask his wife what she thought. Stella was really excited. He had just graduated from university and thought he was going to sell a painting to a very important man. Sadly, it wasn't to be. Hoving called the next day and said that since they were just married and tight on cash, they really couldn't afford the painting right then. Stella was so disappointed that he decided to give the painting away. Today it hangs in the Baltimore Museum of Art. In 1993, the Osaka City Museum of Modern Art purchased one of Stella's *Black Paintings* for $5 million!

Examples of Stella's Black Paintings hang in The Museum of Modern Art (MoMA) in New York City.

Digital Image © 2003 MoMA, N.Y.

curator: *manager of a museum*

 Do you think if something costs a lot of money, it is better than something cheaper? Explain your answer.

Quick Fact
In 1970, Frank Stella was the youngest artist to have a retrospective (exhibition of an artist's life work) at The Museum of Modern Art.

Take Note
We placed *Harran II* at #9 because Stella's shape paintings continued the strong focus on abstraction and influenced artists in many ways.
- If you were opening your own gallery, would you showcase modern artwork like Stella's, or something timeless like the *Mona Lisa*? Explain your answer.

5   4   3   2   1

PHIL–WHITNEY MUSEUM OF AMERICAN ART, NEW YORK

Phil by Chuck Close, 1969

ARTIST: Chuck Close, born 1940

MEDIUM: Synthetic (artificial) polymer on canvas

SIZE: 9 x 7 ft.

WHAT'S NEW: It reinvented portraiture (images of people, usually their faces) and forced the viewer to see the subject matter in a new way.

Funny how the artist's name matches his work! Chuck Close must really be fascinated with faces to make his portraits so big! He wanted the viewer to move in close to his paintings and experience the face as a landscape. Close compares this to "Lilliputians swarming over giants in *Gulliver's Travels*."

When Close painted this portrait of his friend, composer Philip Glass, he was really creating a problem for himself. Most art critics of the time said painting was out of style. But if anyone was painting, abstract expressionism was the style of the day. No artist in his or her right mind would have thought of painting something that people could actually recognize, and certainly not painting a portrait. As far as the art world was concerned, there was nothing modern about portraits.

For this portrait, Close started by photographing Philip Glass. It took him four months to turn the photograph into a painting. Once that was done, he knew he was on to something important. For one thing, he discovered that by recording only what was in the photograph, he was finding totally new shapes and patterns. He had been trying to do this with his earlier abstract paintings, and it just wasn't happening.

Close's larger-than-life portrait made people take notice and look at portraits in a different way. *ARTnews* magazine considers him to be one of the 50 most influential people in

PHIL

BUT WHAT IS IT?

Phil is a large acrylic painting on canvas. It looks like a giant black and white photograph and shows every part of the face in extreme detail. If you stand close to the portrait, it looks abstract. It gradually turns into a face as you move far enough back.

WHERE IS IT NOW?

The Whitney Museum of American Art in New York City purchased the painting of Philip Glass in 1970. Close's work was soon being purchased by museums all over the world.

WHAT'S UP WITH THIS ARTIST?

Close wanted the work to be very large so that the scale of the work would force the viewer to look at the subject matter differently. Here's how he created the portrait:

1. Photograph a model. Make sure the pose is unemotional and the shot is cropped so that only the head is seen.
2. Enlarge the photo and mark a horizontal and vertical grid on top of the photo.
3. Use an extremely large canvas.
4. Translate each little square exactly as it is seen in the photo onto the canvas, square by square.

FOOD FOR THOUGHT

Close was influenced by two things: process art and conceptual art. Process art is a way of making art by following a set of rules. Conceptual art is about ideas rather than feelings. In his art, Close tried to get rid of feelings and focus on an idea that was only in the mind.

Chuck Close's portrait of fellow artist Lucas Samaras really gives an idea of the scale in which Close works.

? Close has said, "Faces are road maps of a life." What do his portraits tell you about his subjects? What would your face say?

Quick Fact

Close's portraits have been compared to mug shots and passport photos. He usually chose to paint people who weren't famous because he wanted the viewer to think about how the portrait was painted, not whom it was of.

The Expert Says...

" American artist Chuck Close has been a leading figure in contemporary art since the early 1970s. ... [Close has] radically changed the definition of modern portraiture. "

— Robert Storr, curator at the Department of Painting and Sculpture at The Museum of Modern Art

Man with a Mission

Chuck Close

Close is seen here working on Elizabeth in his studio in 1989.

In 1988, Close collapsed with a blood clot in his spinal column. It left him paralyzed from the neck down. Close was so consumed by his art that he didn't let his paralysis stop him. Close surprised the art world by returning to painting after his paralysis. He began by holding the paintbrush in his teeth. Eventually he was able to paint with a brush taped onto a hand splint.

Today, Close works in a new way and critics praise his paintings. He still paints huge portraits, but his use of color and soft brushstrokes is entirely new. Roger Angell, writing in *The New Yorker*, said, "A ravaged artist has become, in a miracle, one of the great colorists and brush wielders of his time."

ravaged: *ruined*

Painting in his wheelchair with a brush strapped to his hand, Close is like an art superhero. The paralysis helped him develop a new way of painting. He said, "I tried to imagine what kind of teeny paintings I could make with only that much movement. Even that little bit of neck movement was enough to let me know that perhaps I was not powerless. Perhaps I could do something for myself."

Take Note

We ranked *Phil* #8 because it is a very influential painting that introduced something new and important, and dramatically changed the idea of modern portraiture. However, because it was portraiture, it did not have the same impact on the direction of modern art as the other works ahead of it on this list.
- If an artist wanted to paint your picture, would you allow it? Why or why not?

5   4   3   2   1

An American Tribute to the British People
by Louise Nevelson, 1960–64

ARTIST: Louise Nevelson, 1899–1988

MEDIUM: Wood painted gold

SIZE: 10 x 14 ft.

WHAT'S NEW: It introduced a new form of sculpture and a whole new way of looking at things.

"The freer that women become, the freer men will be. Because when you enslave someone, you are enslaved."

— LOUISE NEVELSON

Louise Nevelson was a very resourceful artist. *An American Tribute to the British People* was created from all kinds of ready-made objects placed into lots of boxes and stacked up to make a sculpture.

It took some time for Nevelson's sculpture to catch people's attention, mostly because she was a woman. Back in the 1950s, some people, including other artists, thought that only men could make real art! Critics dismissed an artwork as soon as they knew a woman had made it.

Nevelson's works are unique because she approached modern sculpture differently from other artists of her day. No one had ever used trash to create art. She was once described as a cross between Catherine the Great and a bag lady because she was always picking up junk and turning it into art. Once she became famous, Nevelson was called the "Empress of Assemblage."

Nevelson was in her 40s before her work was recognized. She continued to work until her death at the age of 88. Today, she is known as one of the foremost sculptors of the second half of the 20th century. Her works are included in over 86 major museum collections around the world.

assemblage: *work of art made by grouping found or unrelated objects*

BUT WHAT IS IT?

An American Tribute to the British People is one of the few sculptures Nevelson painted gold. (Most of her work is black.) It consists of 35 long, narrow boxes joined side by side. It is a huge piece, 10 feet high and 14 feet wide. A lot of wooden objects are arranged inside each box, creating shadows. We chose this piece because of its size, significance, and the fact that Louise used gold paint instead of her usual black. And of course, it was made from trash!

WHERE IS IT NOW?

In 1965, Louise Nevelson presented the sculpture to the Tate Gallery in London, England. The Tate opened in 1897 with only 65 artworks. Today, it has over 65,000 works in its collection, including several by Nevelson.

> **?** Nevelson gave her sculpture to the Tate Gallery in London, England. Do you think this influenced the title of her artwork? Why or why not?

Louise Nevelson

WHAT'S UP WITH THIS ARTIST?

Nevelson worked with wood objects and placed them into boxes to form abstract artworks. She loved them so much that she kept making them until her studio was so full she had to start stacking the boxes on top of one another. Then she had one of those "Aha!" moments when she realized the stacked boxes were a new kind of sculpture. Nevelson rarely made plans or drawings for her sculptures.

> **?** How do you feel about Nevelson's lack of plans? Planning may be important for something like schoolwork, but is it necessary in art?

FOOD FOR THOUGHT

Nevelson was very poor for a long time. However, she was driven to make art. She spent years rooting around the streets of New York looking for interesting materials to use in her art. She would drag what she found back to her studio and then work with it until suddenly the junk became art. In 1979, an outdoor garden in Lower Manhattan was named after her.

Quick Fact

One of Nevelson's largest sculptures, *Sky Gate*, which hung in the World Trade Center, was destroyed along with the twin towers on September 11, 2001.

The Expert Says...

"Her work is … wondrously timeless … Nevelson doesn't ask for interpretation … thereby giving relevance to the most irrelevant object or design."

— Paul Gardner, art critic

7

6

Trash to Treasure

Nevelson may have been poor, but she just had to make art. Her solution? She used stuff other people threw away. Look at this list to see some of the things she turned into art.

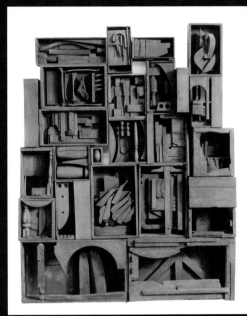

Black Wall, *1959*

- scraps of wood
- boxes and crates
- doorknobs
- pieces of railing
- spindles
- chair legs
- cupboard doors
- jars, vases, and old containers
- tools
- scrap metal

Diminishing Reflection, *1964*

? Imagine you were Nevelson. What "junk" would you use to make something interesting for a project? How would you use it? Why would you use it?

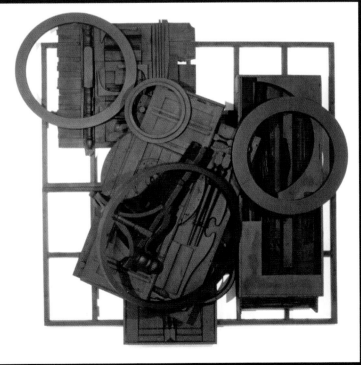

Mirror Shadow VIII, *1985*

Take Note

Louise Nevelson's *An American Tribute to the British People* is ranked #7 because it is an excellent example of Nevelson's special way of making sculpture. It had a very strong influence on female artists and the art world as a whole.

- Imagine that you are an art critic. Keeping in mind the works of art you have read about so far, would you consider Nevelson's sculpture a good example of modern art? Why or why not?

5   4   3   2   1

ST, NUMBER 1

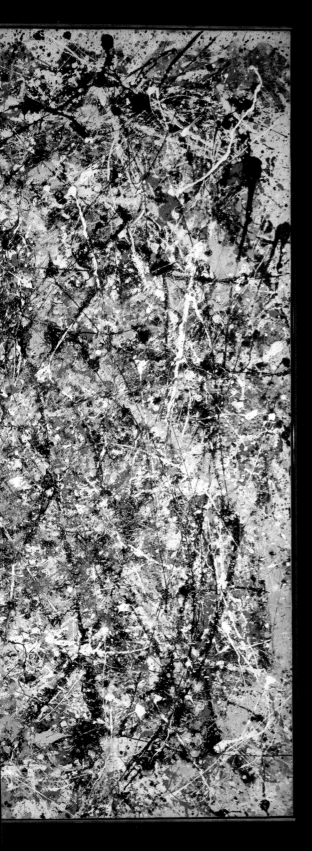

ARTIST: Jackson Pollock, 1912–1956

MEDIUM: Oil, enamel, and aluminum on canvas

SIZE: 7.3 x 9.8 ft.

WHAT'S NEW: It introduced a new style of "action" painting where the artist doesn't follow any rules and anything goes.

"On the floor I am more at ease. I feel nearer, more a part of the painting, since this way I can walk around it, work from the four sides and literally be in the painting."
— JACKSON POLLOCK

Jackson Pollock is one of the most well-known abstract expressionist painters. His work is completely abstract — there is nothing recognizable in it. His paintings are intense and energetic and appear to have been done randomly. The whole point was to express his feelings through paint — he basically let the paint speak for him. In fact, he earned the nickname "Jack the Dripper" because of the way he splashed and dribbled paint on a canvas spread on the floor. This was Pollock's action painting.

In *Lavender Mist, Number 1*, Pollock invented an entirely new way to express his feelings. He spread a huge canvas on the floor of his barn and practically danced on it, throwing and dripping paint all over it. The end result rocked the art world and had everyone talking. This is exactly the kind of art that made people say things like, "A five-year-old could do it!" However, an article about Pollock titled "Is He the Greatest Living Painter in the United States?" appeared in a 1949 edition of *Life* magazine, and he became an instant celebrity — the macho, all-American artist.

macho: *having a strong sense of masculine pride*

LAVENDER MIST, NUMBER 1

BUT WHAT IS IT?

Lavender Mist, Number 1 is a huge painting filled with colored scribble. Spattered lines move all over the place, starting out thickly and slowly trailing off. You can even see handprints near the edges of the painting. It is impossible to look at one spot for long before your eye is pulled in another direction. The painting has an overall pale lavender tone.

WHERE IS IT NOW?

In 1976, the National Gallery of Art in Washington, D.C., purchased the painting. This is where it is usually on display. From time to time, it is lent to other galleries for special shows.

The "Big Dripper" at work!

Quick Fact

In November 2006, Teri Horton, a retired trucker from Costa Mesa, California, discovered that a painting she picked up for $5 in the early 1990s to cheer up a friend may actually be an original Jackson Pollock worth almost $100 million!

WHAT'S UP WITH THIS ARTIST?

Pollock invented his technique in the late 1940s. Like all modern artists, he was competing with Pablo Picasso, who is seen as one of the most important artists of the 20th century. The trouble was, Picasso seemed to have already invented everything in the art world. Then Pollock came up with his idea. Inspired by the sounds of the countryside and jazz, he dripped, dribbled, and poured paint over his canvas. He added new layers over several days until it was complete. And he was on the way to making a name for himself!

 Have you ever been a little competitive with someone else? What did you notice about the situation?

FOOD FOR THOUGHT

Can you believe that scientists have actually studied Pollock's paintings? It turns out that the patterns in Pollock's paintings are fractals — shapes that repeat themselves within the same object. Pollock was trying to paint from his subconscious. He was interested in the idea of chance, but he controlled his movements over the canvas in a sort of dance. He told critics, "I can control the flow of paint. There is no accident."

The Expert Says...

"Your five-year-old could absolutely not do this. But if the art didn't push that button, if it didn't push hard against the notion that … it defied any standard notion of skill, it wouldn't be the modern art that it is.

— Kirk Varnedoe, art historian

10   **9**   **8**   **7**   **6**

COULD A FIVE-YEAR-OLD HAVE DONE IT?

Check out this account and decide for yourself!

With modern art, the artists felt they had to keep coming up with completely new ideas. Can you imagine the pressure? These artists broke all the rules and then left it up to us to decide — is it good or not? Is it even art?

Many people look at Pollock's paintings and wonder if he is really a scam artist. Even Pollock was so caught up in what some of the critics said that he started to wonder if he was a fake!

Pollock seen here in his studio, mid-splatter

Let's check out how Pollock broke the rules ...

1. He placed his canvas on the floor instead of using a traditional easel.

2. He used ordinary house paint instead of using artist's oil paints.

3. He poured or dribbled the paint out of a hole in the can or flicked it with a stick, instead of using a paintbrush.

4. He let other stuff like nails fall into his paintings instead of keeping the surface clean.

5. He walked right onto the surface of his paintings while he worked.

No wonder people were surprised by his work. His process was as rebellious as the finished product!

? What kinds of things do you do that might be seen as "rebellious"?

Take Note

Important art critics think *Lavender Mist, Number 1* is one of Pollock's best works, and we agree. We placed it at #6 because Pollock was incredibly daring in his approach to creating art. He broke all of the rules of how painters should paint and changed people's view of how they saw art.

• Jackson Pollock competed with Pablo Picasso in creating something new. In what ways do you think competition between artists is good?

2   1

Coyote (*also known as* I like America and America Likes Me) *by Joseph Beuys, 1974*

ARTIST: Joseph Beuys (pronounced "boyz"), 1921–1986

MEDIUM: Room, coyote, artist, felt blankets, copper cane, gloves, and 150 *Wall Street Journals*

WHAT'S NEW: It changed the content and purpose of art. It made people think about new possibilities for art.

This is a really strange kind of artwork. It's called "action," or performance, art. This art can portray the actions of an individual or a group. It can happen anywhere, at any time, and for any length of time. The trouble is, once the action is over there is no art to look at anymore. Well, that's not entirely true. You can look at pictures of the action, read descriptions of what happened, and if you're lucky, see a video of it. Still, it does make it pretty hard to figure out if it's really art or not. You have to wonder about this piece. The artist locked himself in a room with a live coyote for three days. That's it.

Some interesting things happened over the three days, and it sure got a lot of attention. But really, is this what you would call art?

You have to understand what Beuys was doing to answer that question. So, what was he doing?

Coyote was action art that took place in May 1974. Beuys flew to New York from Germany. He was wrapped in felt blankets, carried from the plane to a waiting ambulance, and transported to the gallery. Once in the room with the coyote, he repeated a sequence of actions over and over again. After three days, he returned to Germany.

WHERE IS IT NOW?

The performance took place in a small room in a gallery in New York City. It was witnessed by a small group of people, and they then talked to lots of people about it. The estate of Joseph Beuys owns photographs and a 37-minute video of the action. These are all that remain of Beuys's work, other than written descriptions of the event. The objects Beuys used in his actions were often exhibited later as artworks.

> Can you think of an art form — a music video for example — that really got you talking? Explain your answer.

of the mass killing of Native Americans. His action was a way of getting people to pay attention to the wrongs that had been committed in the past. Beuys said, "Basically I'm not that much connected to art. Art interests me only in so far as it gives me the possibility of dialogue with individuals."

In 1962, Beuys joined a group called Fluxus, which is Latin for flow. Fluxus is an international group of artists who combine different artistic media and disciplines and are opposed to traditional ideas of art. They are more interested in artists' opinions, personalities, and actions than in the artworks themselves.

FOOD FOR THOUGHT

Beuys was trying to create an environment that would really shake people up and get them to tap into their spontaneous side. Beuys said, "You could say that a reckoning has to be made with the coyote, and only then can this trauma be lifted." Beuys believed his actions were spiritual experiences for the audience, and that they provided a sense of healing. He is famous for saying, "Everyone is an artist." He meant that people should work creatively, regardless of their jobs.

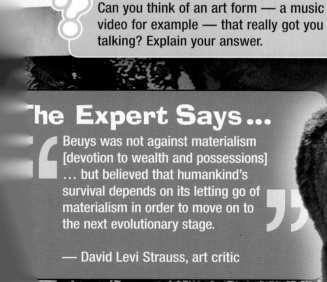

The Expert Says...

" Beuys was not against materialism [devotion to wealth and possessions] … but believed that humankind's survival depends on its letting go of materialism in order to move on to the next evolutionary stage. "

— David Levi Strauss, art critic

THE COYOTE RITUAL

This **account** takes you step-by-step through Beuys's process of creating *Coyote* and explains why he created it.

Joseph Beuys used some symbolic objects — a copper cane, a flashlight, and gloves. Every day 50 copies of *The Wall Street Journal* were delivered to the room. Beuys did certain things over and over again in his interaction with the coyote. These things became the ritual of the performance. Here's what you would have seen:

1. Beuys strikes the musical triangle that is hanging around his neck.

2. A recording of a loud turbo engine begins to play outside the enclosure.

3. Beuys pulls on his gloves.

4. Beuys wraps himself in a heavy felt blanket so it looks as if he is inside a teepee.

5. Beuys sticks the crook of his cane out the top of his teepee and points it at the coyote.

6. Beuys bends and moves as the coyote moves, always keeping the crook of his cane pointed at the coyote.

7. Every once in awhile Beuys falls to the ground as though he's in a trance.

The curious coyote checks out Beuys who is wrapped in a blanket.

The whole ritual was Beuys's way of channeling the coyote's energy.

Through *Coyote*, Beuys wanted to portray the kinds of things that people were doing to damage the world. Before Europeans arrived in America, Native Americans considered the coyote a powerful god. Europeans considered it a pest and tried to kill it. Beuys saw the coyote as a symbol of how the American continent and Native cultures had been harmed by the European settlers.

Beuys kept his ritual going for three days so that people would be able to have enough time to really get a sense of the coyote. By the time it was over, a real bond between the coyote and Beuys seemed to have developed.

Should *Coyote* be considered art? What makes something art?

Quick Fact

Coyote is the "trickster/transformer" in Native American culture. According to the Navajo, "the spirit of coyote is so mighty that the human being cannot understand what it is, or what it can do for mankind in the future."

Take Note

We ranked *Coyote* #5 because this work was a dramatic change of direction for artists. Beuys influenced how people think about the way we live and what we will need to survive in the future. However, *Coyote* is not well known in North America, so its influence among the general population and on artists is not as great as those ahead of it in this list.

• Compare *Coyote* to #10, *Valley Curtain*. How are the two artworks similar? How are they different?

5   4   3   2   1

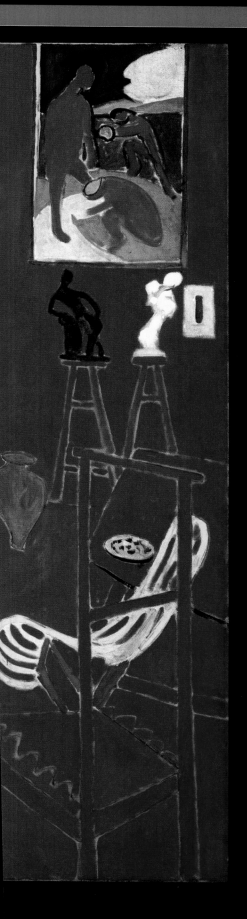

ARTIST: Henri Matisse, 1869–1954

MEDIUM: Oil on canvas

SIZE: 5.9 x 7.2 ft.

WHAT'S NEW: Its use of such a large area of bold, vibrant color and the way it played with space were very influential in 20th century painting.

According to Russian critic Jacob Tugenhold, "Matisse is the greatest colorist of our time, and the most cultivated: he has absorbed into himself all the luxury of the East and of Byzantium (Biz-an-tee-um)." This quote proves Matisse's love of Islamic art. Matisse wanted to combine the ideas of flatness and pattern that he saw in Islamic art with his love of color. His pictures look deceptively simple, but don't be fooled — he worked and struggled with them to get to that sense of simplicity. In *Red Studio,* he changed the background several times before being satisfied that red was the best choice. The way Matisse uses red in *Red Studio* makes everything seem flat. He even floods the furniture with red — what looks like lines are really just gaps in the red paint and the yellow or blue can be seen underneath.

Matisse was the leader of the "Fauves," French for "wild beasts." Just to be nasty, critics gave the name Fauves to painters who used color so expressively. It's a funny name for Matisse, though. He deliberately tried to create art that made people feel good.

Can you figure this picture out? Why on earth did we rank it #4 on our list?

Byzantium: *ancient city and empire, whose art and architecture were very decorative*

Quick Fact

Check out the chair in the foreground. That's a special kind of chair in the lower right corner of *Red Studio.* The chair is made for paintings, not for sitting. Different sizes of paintings can be placed on the chair, and the teeth separate the paintings from one another.

RED STUDIO

BUT WHAT IS IT?

Red Studio is a large oil painting of Matisse's own studio. However, it's like an Alice in Wonderland version of the real thing. The pictures and sculptures are Matisse's, and almost everything else is art or craft. It is a kind of escape from the real world.

WHERE IS IT NOW?

The painting is at The Museum of Modern Art in New York City. For years, it hung in London in a nightclub. An American saw it in 1945 and bought it for £600 (almost $1200). It was purchased by The Museum of Modern Art not long after that and permanently installed in the museum in 1949. Because works of art in museums are rarely sold, you could say that today it is priceless.

WHAT'S UP WITH THIS ARTIST?

In 1952, Matisse decided to honor his birthplace in France. He donated some of his works and set up a museum there. This is one of very few museums created by an artist in his own lifetime. When he was old and too weak to stand at a canvas and paint, he started making collages. He would "draw" with scissors, cutting out bright paper shapes and getting his assistant to attach them to brilliant backgrounds.

FOOD FOR THOUGHT

Matisse is considered one of the most influential artists of his time. In 1954, a famous American painter named Mark Rothko painted *Homage to Matisse*, which sold in a 2005 auction for $22,416,000. Rothko said he spent hours and hours sitting in front of *Red Studio* and that he would "become" the color.

> Many artists have studied *Red Studio* intensively to try to understand what Matisse was doing. Mark Rothko said he "became" the color as he looked at the painting. What do you think Rothko meant by this?

> *Red Studio* is a real place, but Matisse doesn't show how it really looks. He shows how he feels about the studio. Do you like the way Matisse portrays the studio? Why?

Quick Fact

Matisse believed that painting could provide a kind of escape from the world. He wanted his art to have the "effect of a good armchair on a tired businessman."

The Expert Says...

" I paid endless visits to the Redfern Gallery in order to absorb ... this great masterpiece. It was the most influential painting in my entire career. "

— Patrick Heron, famous British artist

Matisse vs Picasso

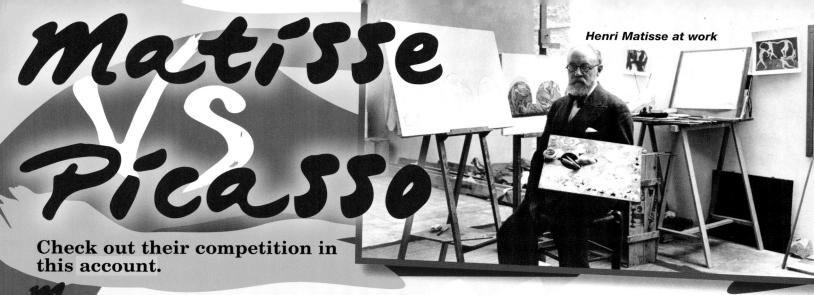

Henri Matisse at work

Check out their competition in this account.

Matisse was already the most famous painter in Paris when Pablo Picasso first arrived from Spain. Matisse was 36 and Picasso was 25. In 1906, Leo and Gertrude Stein, important art collectors, introduced the two artists. From then on, Picasso and Matisse were pretty much in open competition. Picasso would respond to what Matisse did, and Matisse would do something even more avant-garde — back and forth like a Ping-Pong game. The competition between one another forced them to continue to develop new techniques.

An interesting thing about this time was how each artist attracted fiercely loyal followers. In 1907, the artists exchanged paintings. When Picasso hung Matisse's painting in his studio, his friends threw suction cup darts at it to show their support for Picasso.

Later in life, the two men became friends and when Matisse died, Picasso spent two years painting canvas after canvas that seemed to be trying to bring Matisse back. Today, the two artists continue to be competitors in auctions and their works are often placed side by side in catalogs or on display.

Both Picasso and Matisse remain popular. Picasso is the leader when it comes to the price of his paintings. In an auction on November 8, 2000, one of his paintings sold for $50,000,000! The next day, a Matisse sold for $15,000,000. When we look at drawings, though, it's a different story. Matisse's drawings have been getting nearly twice the price of Picasso's since 2002. Matisse's prints are also more popular with investors, getting higher prices at sales.

Pablo Picasso in his studio

Matisse's paintings sell for a lot of money. Do you think that makes them great art? Explain.

Take Note

We ranked *Red Studio* #4 because it inspired artists to work with color in totally new ways and led to a whole new style called Color Field painting.
- Work with a partner to compare *Red Studio* with *Lavender Mist, Number 1*. Does one work seem easier to understand than the other? Do you think this makes any difference in the work's ability to influence others? Explain your answer.

avant-garde: *experimental; daring (French word meaning "vanguard" — leaders of a movement)*

5   **4**   3   2   1

MARILYN DIP

MARILYN DIPTYCH–TATE GALLERY, LONDON/ART RESOURCE,NY

Marilyn Diptych *by Andy Warhol, 1962*

TYCH

ARTIST: Andy Warhol, 1928–1987

MEDIUM: Acrylic and silk screen (a method of printmaking in which a design is imposed on a screen of silk and ink is forced through the screen onto the printing surface) on canvas

SIZE: 6.7 x 4.8 ft.

WHAT'S NEW: It pushed people to think about the subject matter in art differently. It introduced the idea of the mass production of art.

"In the future, everybody will be world-famous for 15 minutes."

- Andy Warhol

Marilyn Monroe was someone larger than life. After her death in August 1962, Andy Warhol couldn't resist painting her picture. It was as if he wanted to pay tribute to her. He used a publicity photograph from her 1953 film *Niagara*, and just kept playing around with it, changing colors and printing it over and over again.

Some critics say Warhol is one of the most influential artists of the second half of the 20th century. *Marilyn Diptych* represents one of art's turning points because it changed the way artists saw and did things. Warhol's art focuses on popular culture. This piece represents Marilyn Monroe the star, not the person.

How can a painting that just shows copies of a photograph over and over again be so influential that it ranks #3 on our list?

Diptych: pair of paintings on two panels, linked by theme

 Warhol used someone else's photograph to make his painting of Marilyn Monroe. How do you feel about this idea? Does it make his art better or worse than an artist whose work is completely original? Explain your reasoning.

MARILYN DIPTYCH

BUT WHAT IS IT?

Marilyn Diptych is a huge, two-panel silk screen painting. It is in the pop art style and repeats the same picture of Marilyn Monroe 50 times. Half the painting is in color and the other half in black and white.

WHERE IS IT NOW?

The painting is in London, England. In 1980, the Tate Collection bought *Marilyn Diptych* for £100,000 (around $193,575). The Tate estimates that today the painting would probably cost between £25 and £30 million (around $48.4 to $129.7 million).

WHAT'S UP WITH THIS ARTIST?

Warhol always had a fascination with death and celebrity. He liked to combine these two themes in all of his artwork. Ironically, in 1968 a woman walked into Warhol's studio and shot him three times in the chest. He was rushed to the hospital and pronounced dead. But when doctors massaged his heart, he came back to life. Although he painted *Marilyn Diptych* before this incident, the combination of death and celebrity is still clear in the painting.

 Why do you think some people are fascinated by celebrities and by death?

FOOD FOR THOUGHT

The media called Warhol the "Prince of Pop." The whole purpose of pop art was to take the things we see as part of everyday life and turn them into "high art." At the time, Warhol's paintings made people question the difference between pop culture and art.

This is a silk-screened self-portrait of Andy Warhol.

The Expert Says...

" It would be an enormous claim to say he invented celebrity. But I think what he did — as any artist does — was to articulate it through visual imagery. He had a capacity to sense what was in the public consciousness and he seized on that. "

— Donna De Salvo, curator, Tate Modern

articulate: *express*

A Priceless Find

An article from _Varsity_, by Aidan Johnson

Lasalle Secondary School in Sudbury, Ontario, [Canada], did what countless art lovers only dream about: they found a Warhol silk screen portrait of Marilyn Monroe in their vaults.

The piece had hung forgotten in a meeting room for nearly three decades, a psychedelic relic from some bygone era when schools had money. After Sotheby's auction confirmed its worth to be between $15,000 and $18,600, Lasalle principal Bert Brankley had these words:

"It sounds crass, but when I looked at that piece of art, I said to myself, 'That's the better part of a computer lab.'"

Excuse me? Feasting your eyes on Marilyn Monroe and only thinking of the letters IBM? That isn't just crass: it's sacrilegious. This guy's attitude reminds me of a drooling cartoon wolf out of Looney Toons, staring at Porky Pig and seeing nothing but a ham sandwich with extra mayo.

The tragedy of Lasalle's decision is that the school lost the opportunity to carry an artwork produced by an artist whose work is ripe for

piquing students' interests. Warhol's obsession with pop and consumer culture puts him in synch with the TV-teethed brains of modern teenagers. His omnipresent images make him one of the most accessible artists of the visual canon. Maybe that's why Sister Wendy [British art expert] calls his work "unforgettable." For in all his artificial glory, Warhol is the way to fix our turbulent 20th century in the imaginations of the 21st.

"When I got my first TV set," Warhol once remarked, "I stopped caring so much about having a close relationship."

---

crass: _rude_
sacrilegious: _disrespectful_

TV-teethed: _raised on frequent TV watching_
omnipresent: _everywhere at once_
canon: _artworks considered to be the best by critics_

Quick Fact

Warhol had several assistants who made his silk screen prints. He gave them directions to follow and they made the different versions and variations.

? Warhol made no secret about the fact that he had staff to do his paintings. The paintings were his ideas, but he didn't really make them. Are they still his art? Why or why not?

Take Note

Marilyn Diptych is considered one of Andy Warhol's best works, which is why we ranked it #3. By using everyday images and focusing on popular celebrities, Warhol made people think that everything can be art and that everyone can be an artist. This idea was much more modern than Matisse's _Red Studio_.

• Take a simple photograph of yourself with a white background and make several copies of the photo. Use markers or watercolor paints to play with your image the way Warhol did. Once it is completed, sit and look at it from a distance. Do you think your work is art? Explain your answer.

5   4   **3**   2   1

Guernica by Pablo Picasso, 1937

On April 27, 1937, Guernica, the oldest town in the northern Basque region of Spain, was bombed. The air raid was carried out by Nazi Germany, which was fighting with the Nationalists during the Spanish Civil War. In less than four hours, almost one-third of the townspeople were killed. Picasso started painting *Guernica* four days later. *Guernica* does not show an eyewitness account of the

bombing with planes or bombs. Instead, Picasso chose images that he had used before to symbolize Spain — the horse, the bull, the tiled roofs, and the weeping women. He combined them in a dramatic painting that shows the horrors and timelessness of war.

Nationalists: *military group led by the dictator Francisco Franco*

ARTIST: Pablo Picasso, 1881–1973

MEDIUM: Oil on canvas

SIZE: 11.5 x 25.5 ft.

WHAT'S NEW: It is the most important antiwar artwork of the 20th century. It made people realize that modern art could deal with historical events.

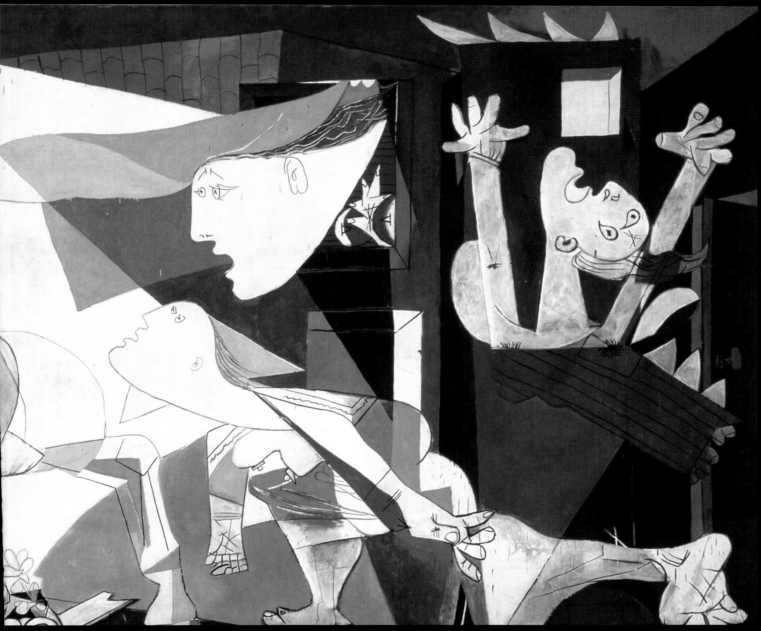

The first reactions to *Guernica* were negative. It was described by one critic as a "hodgepodge of body parts that any four-year-old could have painted." However, many people felt differently, and, as early as 1938, *Guernica* was described as a masterpiece. They felt *Guernica* was a great representation of the destruction of the city. It hung in The Museum of Modern Art in New York City for over 40 years. There it gained the reputation as one of the most important artworks of the century.

hodgepodge: *mixed-up combination*

GUERNICA—ART RESOURCE, NY

GUERNICA

BUT WHAT IS IT?

Guernica is a huge oil painting. It shows a political event from the point of view of the victims. The scale of the painting reinforces the devastation caused by the bombing. It has come to stand for peace. Picasso painted in the cubist style. In cubist artworks, objects are broken up, analyzed, and reassembled in an abstract form. The artist illustrates the subject from many viewpoints to present the piece in a greater perspective.

 Can you visualize how big this mural is? Measure it out on your classroom wall to see for yourself.

WHERE IS IT NOW?

Picasso made it clear that *Guernica* was not to be sent to Spain until democracy and freedom had been restored. As a result, after the Paris International Exposition (World's Fair), *Guernica* toured Europe and America to warn people about the threat of fascism. The painting was returned to Spain in 1981. It is now displayed in the Museo Nacional Centro de Arte Reina Sofia in Madrid, the capital of Spain.

fascism: *system of rule where the government has total control but allows private ownership of property*

Do you think *Guernica* is famous because it is a great painting, or is it a great painting because it is so famous? Explain.

WHAT'S UP WITH THIS ARTIST?

In 1937, Picasso was asked to paint a mural for the World's Fair. He had been trying to come up with an idea for three months. When news of the bombing of Guernica reached Paris, more than a million protesters filled the streets. Inspired by the stark black and white photographs and energy of the crowd, Picasso rushed angrily to his studio and started working on the mural. It took Picasso just over a month to complete the mural.

FOOD FOR THOUGHT

Cubism introduced the idea of "art for art's sake," abstract art, and modern art. *Guernica* was the first cubist painting that dealt with a historical event. When asked to explain the symbolism in *Guernica*, Picasso said, "It is not up to the painter to define the symbols. Otherwise it would be better if he wrote them out in so many words! The public who looks at the picture must interpret the symbols as they understand them."

Quick Fact

Many residents of Guernica think the painting should be housed in the new Guggenheim Museum Bilbao, which is only 20 minutes from the town of Guernica. They are bitter that it is in Madrid.

Picasso is pictured here painting Guernica.

10   9   8   7

A Work in Progress

Check out this photo essay showing how Picasso created *Guernica*.

Picasso began by drawing small planning sketches. He kept changing his mind and playing with the composition. Finally, on May 11, 1937, Picasso started to draw the actual mural on the canvas.

Picasso worked furiously for the next six days. He started to fill in areas of light and dark and added more details. Notice the changes in this photo of the work in progress. Note the dark shape between the mother and the child on the far left. Do you think it could stand for something? What could it be?

 What specific images make this painting powerful?

The Expert Says...

 Guernica has become for people around the world visceral, visual evidence of the true nature of war. ...

— Russell Martin, cultural historian

visceral: *emotional*

Take Note

We placed Picasso's *Guernica* at #2 because it is an excellent example of cubism, a style that influenced artists to keep looking for different ways to make art. This artwork also got a lot of people talking about its controversial images, much more so than Warhol's *Marilyn Diptych*.

• Choose another tragedy in history that you would like to see painted in a cubist way. Why would you choose this tragedy, and what would you hope to accomplish through this painting?

5   **4**   **3**   **2**   **1**

A 1964 replica of Marcel Duchamp's 1917 Fountain

ARTIST: Marcel Duchamp, 1887–1968

MEDIUM: Glazed ceramic with black paint

SIZE: 15 x 19 x 25 in.

WHAT'S NEW: It completely changed the way people think of art and introduced readymade art — and led to important innovations in 20th century sculpture.

This might look like a common urinal to you, but in 1917, it became art!

Marcel Duchamp (Mar-sell Du-shohn) bought the urinal from a company called J.L. Mott Iron Works in New York. He took it back to his studio and turned it 90 degrees from its normal position. Duchamp signed it "R. Mutt 1917." He called it *Fountain* and entered it into an unjuried art exhibition. Even though the Society of Independent Artists said they would exhibit all work submitted, they immediately rejected Duchamp's entry. They said it wasn't art.

So how did this urinal become #1 on our list? Turn the page to find out how it became one of the most famous pieces of art in the 20th century.

unjuried: *not judged or evaluated*

If you wanted to make a statement about art, what sort of everyday object would you choose?

FOUNTAIN

BUT WHAT IS IT?

Fountain is what Marcel Duchamp called a readymade sculpture. A ready-made is work of art made from an everyday, mass-produced object that the artist chooses and turns into art. *Fountain* is an ordinary urinal, laid flat on its back and signed "R. Mutt 1917." But it is no longer a urinal because Duchamp has signed it and given it a title. He makes us think about it — and about art — in a new way by giving the object a new meaning.

WHERE IS IT NOW?

No one knows where the original is. It was lost soon after it was made. Replicas are in the San Francisco Museum of Modern Art, the National Gallery of Canada in Ottawa, Canada, the Kyoto Museum in Japan, the Foundation Dina Vierny in Paris, and the Indiana University Art Museum in Bloomington. One of the artist's proofs is in the Musée National d'Art Moderne at the Centre Pompidou in Paris. Some of the replicas are in private collections.

Quick Fact

The original *Fountain* was lost and only a 1917 photograph taken by Alfred Stieglitz shows what it really looked like. Duchamp authorized 11 replicas, or copies, of *Fountain* to be made: one in 1950, one in 1953, one in 1963, and an edition of eight in 1964. He also allowed two artist's proofs to be made. Each of the replicas made in 1964 has an important brass plaque that identifies it as part of the signed and numbered edition of eight.

People paid over a million dollars for copies of the original *Fountain*. Do you think they were buying real art? Why or why not?

WHAT'S UP WITH THIS ARTIST?

Marcel Duchamp was a founding member of the Society of Independent Artists, a group that said they believed in the open and free display of art. Duchamp wanted to see if they really meant it so he came up with the idea of *Fountain*. Did that ever cause a fuss! The Society claimed *Fountain* was neither decent nor art, and they refused to show it. Duchamp resigned from the Society and wrote an article called "The Richard Mutt Case" defending the work. *Fountain* sparked a huge scandal in the art world, and people have been arguing about it ever since.

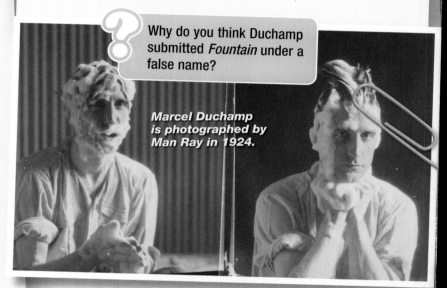
Why do you think Duchamp submitted *Fountain* under a false name?

Marcel Duchamp is photographed by Man Ray in 1924.

FOOD FOR THOUGHT

Fountain continues to be very controversial. It challenged conventional thinking and sparked a whole new way of making art. It showed that art can be valuable because of its ideas. It doesn't matter what it looks like as long as you get the message. Almost 90 years after it was made, *Fountain* continues to get people excited and make them question their traditional ideas. In a 1999 auction, one of the 1964 replicas of *Fountain* sold to a Greek collector, Dimitri Daskalopoulos, for $1,762,500. He said he bought it because, "For me, *Fountain* represents the origins of contemporary art." In 2004, *Fountain* was named the most influential modern artwork of all time by 500 experts.

THE RICHARD MUTT CASE

May 1917
By Beatrice Wood, H.-P. Roché, and Marcel Duchamp

Check out this excerpt from the article shown at right …

They say any artist paying six dollars may exhibit. Mr. Richard Mutt sent in a fountain. Without discussion this article disappeared and was never exhibited.

What were the grounds for refusing Mr. Mutt's fountain:

1. Some contend it was immoral, vulgar.
2. Others, it was plagiarism, a plain piece of plumbing.

Now Mr. Mutt's fountain is not immoral, that is absurd, no more than a bathtub is immoral. It is a fixture that you see every day in plumbers' show windows.

Whether Mr. Mutt with his own hands made the fountain or not has no importance. He CHOSE it. He took an ordinary article of life, placed it so that its useful significance disappeared under new title and point of view, and created a new thought for that object.

As for plumbing, that is absurd. The only works of art America has given are her plumbing and her bridges.

---

vulgar: *crude and offensive*
plagiarism: *copying someone else's work as a form of stealing*

THE BLIND MAN

The Richard Mutt Case

The Expert Says…

" The Duchampian notion that art can be made of anything has finally taken off. … [T]here is a new generation out there saying, 'Duchamp opened up modern art.' "

— Simon Wilson, art expert

Quick Fact

Later in Duchamp's life, he stated, "You can make people swallow anything; that's what happened with *Fountain*."

Do you think Duchamp was being sincere in his art, or was he trying to prove that people will call anything art? Explain your answer.

Take Note

Duchamp's *Fountain* ranks #1 on our list because it marks a real turning point in art. *Fountain* influenced the way artists thought about art for the rest of the century. No other artwork on this list had the same impact as *Fountain*.

• Compare Picasso's ideas with Duchamp's and decide who really paved the way for modern art. Support your decision with evidence found in this book.

5   4   3   2   1

We Thought ...

Here are the criteria we used in ranking the 10 most provocative artworks of the 20th century.

The work of art:
- Was creative
- Was original
- Was daring
- Had a big influence on the art world
- Stirred up a lot of excitement
- Sold for a lot of money
- Changed the way artists created their works
- Changed the way people thought of and valued art
- Portrayed art outside of museums and galleries
- Proved critics wrong

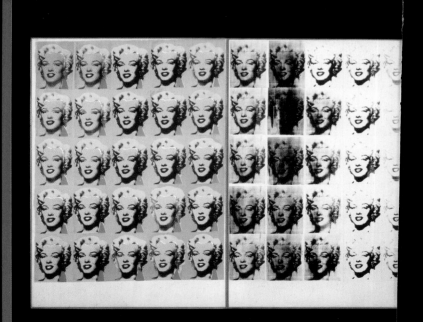

Index